# 50 Needlepoint Stitches

This comprehensive book of fifty canvas stitches will be useful not only to teachers and students but to all women who are interested in canvas embroidery. The stitches range from those of simple straight-forward structure to composite stitches incorporating two or more shades of thread. The correct working method of each stitch is clearly shown in diagrammatic form, with text and close-up photograph. In addition, the given stitches may also be used with minimum adaptation for various other types of counted thread embroidery on evenweave fabrics.

This title was published in England as
*50 Canvas Embroidery Stitches*

1 3 5 7 9 11 13 15 17 19 M/P 20 18 16 14 12 10 8 6 4 2

Printed in the United States of America
Library of Congress Catalog Card Number 77-80339

ISBN 0-684-14786-6

# Useful Information

## Points to be noted for working on Canvas

1 If possible, buy all yarn at one time, particularly yarn for a background or large area worked in one colour.

2 Use a square or oblong frame, never a circular embroidery frame.

3 When calculating the amount of canvas required for any item, add an extra 5 to 7·5 cm (2 to 3 in) of canvas all round to allow for stretching and mounting.

4 Make every stitch in two movements.

5 Work to an even tension, do not pull the thread too tightly.

6 Keep the back of the work smooth and free from knots.

7 Never have more than 45 cm (18 in) of Tapisserie Wool in the needle.

8 When commencing at the centre of a plain area of tapestry worked in Trammed Gros Point Stitch or Trammed Straight Gobelin Stitch, make certain that the Trammed Split Stitches are staggered and cross the central line (see pages 9 and 10). This also applies to any stitch used to cover a large area in one colour, varying lengths of thread should be used so that the beginning and end of the threads do not start or finish on the same vertical line, thus avoiding a noticeable ridge created as the work progresses.

# Materials and Equipment

## Canvas

Canvas embroidery is worked by counting the threads of the canvas and working each stitch over the stated number of threads therefore an evenweave canvas must be used. There are various types of canvas, single thread, double thread, fine and heavy. The type of canvas required will depend upon the thickness of embroidery thread to be used. It is advisable to purchase the best quality canvas available as this will be the foundation of your work. This canvas is made from what are known as polished threads, which are smooth and rounded. Canvas made from this type of thread is firm and does not readily twist out of shape.

Single Thread Canvas and Double Thread Canvas are generally available in various widths, Single Thread Canvas having an exact number of threads, and Double Thread Canvas having an exact number of holes to the centimetre (inch) each way of the canvas.

There is a wide range of canvas available covering the requirements for all types of canvas embroidery, from very fine work

A

B

C

4

using fine threads, to rich textured effects using thick yarns. Choose canvas type and width according to the article being made and calculate the quantity required. ALWAYS ALLOW A MARGIN OF 5 TO 7·5 cm (2 to 3 in) EXTRA CANVAS ALL ROUND. This is necessary for the final stretching and mounting. Your local Needlework Shop will advise you with regard to the most suitable canvas for your purpose.

## Frames

All canvas work should be mounted on a square or oblong frame, never a round frame. These frames generally consist of two rollers, each with a piece of tape firmly nailed along its length. One type of frame has slots in the ends of the rollers into which two side laths fit. Each lath has holes at regular intervals at the ends and pegs or screws fit into the holes to keep the frame stretched. There are slight variations to the method of assembly as described above – see illustrations. It is essential that the size of frame should be correct. As a guide, the width of the canvas should fit the tape on the rollers with little adjustment. It is easier to adjust a larger sized frame to many canvas sizes and this is, therefore, more useful. The illustrations show the various types of frame available. The length of canvas can be rolled and adjusted accordingly.

**A** Tapestry Floor Frame : available in various widths. This frame is particularly useful as it stands by itself and can be placed in any suitable position.

**B** Tapestry Threaded Side Hand Frame with adjustable wooden sides : available in various widths. This frame requires to be supported at each side at a comfortable working height. This leaves both hands free – one hand to work on top of the frame, the other below. This is explained in more detail in the section on Stitches – Two-hand Work Method.

**C** Tapestry Rotating Frame : available in various widths. This frame has a depth of 30 cm (12 in) and therefore has the advantage of being easy to carry. However, should the article to be embroidered be longer than 30 cm (12 in), the lacing will have to be repeated each time the canvas is re-rolled. This frame also requires to be supported at each side when in use.

Your local Needlework Shop will advise you with regard to the most suitable frame for your purpose.

## Assembling the Canvas on the Frame

The canvas should be mounted on any type of frame in the following manner:

1 Mark the centre of canvas lengthwise and widthwise with a line of basting stitches and mark the centre of the tapes with a pencil.

2 Fold down 1·5 cm ($\frac{1}{2}$ in) of the cut edges of the canvas and sew securely to the tape on the rollers which lie at the top and bottom of the frame. If required, turn in the selvedge sides to fit tapes. The centre pencil marks on the tapes should be matched to the centre basting stitches on the canvas when sewing the canvas to the tapes.

3 Wind the surplus canvas round the rollers, assemble the frame and adjust the screws to that the canvas is stretched taut from top to bottom.

4 The sides of the canvas are now laced round the laths with fine string or 4 strands of button thread; if fine canvas is used, stitch tape to the free sides then lace.

NOTE: In the case of very wide or extra long articles it may be necessary to mount the canvas in the frame with the narrow width to the tapes. This may, in some instances, mean that the selvedges and not the cut edges are sewn to the tapes. As this is an exception to the rule, fixed frames such as the Floor Frame may not be suitable, as it frequently means that the embroiderer must work with the frame in the "side-on" position to allow the stitches to be worked and lie in the correct way according to the choice of design or the effect desired.

## Embroidery Threads

The threads normally used for canvas embroidery depend largely on the finished purpose of the embroidery. It is essential that the embroidery thread is suitable to the type of canvas used, thick enough to cover the canvas thread completely but not so thick as to create difficulty in passing the threaded needle through the canvas which results in distorting the canvas weave. Whenever possible, it is advisable to purchase a large quantity of one shade of thread at the same time, e.g. for the background, as any slight change in the dye lots might be noticeable in the finished work.

The following list of threads are suitable and may be used in the manufactured thicknesses for most types of fine/medium weight canvas. However, if a heavier type of canvas is used with fewer holes or threads to the centimetre (inch) it may be found that two or more thicknesses will be required to cover the canvas thread completely. Work a trial piece before commencing the main piece of embroidery to establish the best number of thicknesses to use.

Coats Anchor Tapisserie Wool : This wool is a firm, well twisted yarn, moth-resistant, colour fast and washable, although when used on canvas the article should be dry cleaned (see Dry Cleaning paragraph). There is a wide variety of shades ranging from the subtle tones of conventional tapestry shades to the vivid colour suitable for modern embroidery. Tapisserie Wool is available in 13 m 71 cm (15 yd) skeins with a range of 220 fast-dyed shades : 39 of these shades are produced in 28·35 gram (1 oz) hanks, with an additional 7 shades supplied only in hanks. These 46 hanks are known as grounding wools. Each hank contains 82 m 26 cm (90 yd) and can be used when a considerable number of skeins are required and they are most useful when a large area of background has to be covered. It is recommended that there should not be more than 45 cm (18 in) of Tapisserie Wool in the needle in order to prevent the wool fraying, caused by friction when it is pulled repeatedly through the holes of the canvas. Change the position of the wool in the eye of the needle occasionally, to avoid friction.

Clark's Anchor Soft Embroidery : A fairly thick, soft thread with a matt finish. It is available in 9 m (10 yd) skeins in white, black and a range of colours.

Clark's Anchor Stranded Cotton : This thread is a loosely twisted thread with a lustrous mercerised finish. It consists of six strands which can easily be separated and used singly or in groups of two, three or more strands (nine is equivalent to the thickness of Tapisserie Wool). It is a versatile colour fast thread suitable for most types of embroidery, produced in 8 m (8½ yd) skeins which are available in white, black and an extensive range of shades.

Clark's Anchor Pearl Cotton No. 8 : This thread is suitable for medium/fine embroidery having a lustrous finish with a well-defined twist, which produces a slightly embossed effect on finished work. It is produced in 84 m (92 yd) 10 gram balls in white, black and a range of colours.

Clark's Anchor Coton à Broder : This is a single thread with a highly twisted lustrous finish. Skeins are available in white, black and a range of colours. The dolled skeins can be opened out and easily cut to provide a number of 45 cm (18 in) lengths which is especially convenient for school use.

## Needles

For canvas embroidery a needle with a rounded point is always used.

Milward International Range tapestry needles are available in three sizes for different thicknesses of thread :

No. 18 for Tapisserie Wool and 9 strands of Stranded Cotton.
No. 20 for 6 strands of Stranded Cotton.
No. 24 for 2, 3 and 4 strands of Stranded Cotton and Pearl Cotton No. 8.
The important points to remember are:– a) The eye of the needle is sufficiently large to enable the thickness of thread to pass through easily without causing the thread to fray and b) The threaded needle must not be too thick, otherwise the canvas threads will be forced apart.

### Scissors
These should be sharp with pointed blades suitable for trimming away surplus threads.

### Thimble
A thimble is useful for embroidery to protect the middle finger when pushing the needle through the canvas. Buy a good quality one in metal (preferably silver) and make sure that if fits well.

### Starting and finishing off threads
To commence or finish threads in canvas work, do not use knots, as they stand out in relief when the work is finally stretched and mounted. To commence an area of canvas needlework, push the needle and thread through the canvas on the right side, about 5 cm (2 in) from the point of working, leaving a short end of thread. When the length of thread is almost finished, darn in 2 cm ($\frac{3}{4}$ in) of the end on the wrong side and cut away surplus; darn in the original end left at the beginning on the wrong side, but not where a thread has been previously darned.

## Stitches

### Two-hand Work Method
When canvas is correctly stretched on the frame it is impossible to make any stitch in one movement, although for the purpose of the diagrams the stitches are shown in this way with the needle entering into, and emerging from the canvas at the same time. With a little experience, speed and regularity of stitch can be obtained by using both hands. The method is as follows: with one hand on top of the frame, insert the needle downwards through the canvas and pull the needle through with the other hand below the frame then push the needle upwards through the canvas and pull the needle up and out with the first hand. Continue in this way being careful to work to an even tension,

do not pull the thread too tightly.

## Stitch Diagrams

All the stitch diagrams have been illustrated on single thread canvas with the exception of Trammed Gros Point Stitch which is illustrated on double thread canvas. Many of the stitches may be adapted to suit double thread canvas but care should be taken to ensure that the surface of the canvas is completely covered. The number of threads over which each stitch formation is shown can be altered to suit the design and purpose.

In itself Split Trammed Stitch is not a canvas stitch but it is recommended that it be used when working Gros Point Stitch on double thread canvas. It ensures that the canvas threads are completely covered not only giving better wearing qualities to the finished work, but also giving a richer appearance. All Trammed Stitches should be of the same colour as the surface Gros Point Stitch. The following diagrams show the method of working Split Trammed Stitch on Double and Single thread canvas.

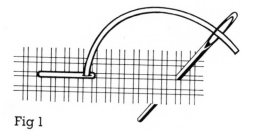

## Fig 1

Double Thread Canvas. Fig. 1 the thread is brought through at the intersection where a pair of narrow vertical threads cross a pair of narrow horizontal threads. It is carried along the required distance (no longer than 13 cm (5 in)) and passed through the canvas at a similar intersection of threads.

**Continued overleaf**

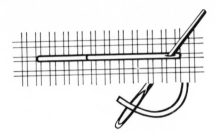

**Fig 2**

Fig. 2 bring the thread through 1 vertical thread to the left on the same line, piercing the stitch just made, thus forming a Split Stitch. Each Trammed Stitch must be placed in such a way that the stitches do not start or finish at the same pair of vertical threads.

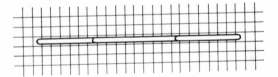

**Fig 3**

Single Thread Canvas. Occasionally it is advisable to tram single thread canvas where complete coverage of the canvas is required e.g. Straight Gobelin Stitch (see page 46). The method used is similar to that described for double thread canvas, the principal difference is in the construction of the canvas, see Fig. 3, otherwise the stitches are worked in the same way with 2 horizontal canvas threads left between rows.

# Canvas Designs

## Prepared Canvas Designs

If a needlework tapestry kit is used the embroiderer is normally supplied with full working instructions, a prepared canvas either with the design stencilled or trammed ready to be worked and the necessary quantity of threads and needle to complete the article. The appropriate thread colours are then matched up to the corresponding colour guide at the side or the trammed threads on the prepared canvas.

## Chart Designs

Another method of working a canvas design is to work following a chart, sign key and detailed instructions. The embroiderer purchases separately, all the materials required. Usually one square on the chart represents one stitch but this largely depends on the canvas stitches used, variations do occur, when for instance Cross Stitch is used it may be worked over two, three or four canvas threads, in this case one square would still represent one stitch but would also represent two, three or four threads each way of the canvas. The instructions must be followed carefully. The symbols (signs) represent the colours used and a sign key is given to be used in conjunction with the chart.

## Transferring Original Designs

By far the most rewarding method of producing a design, is to create one's own. Even if one does not have the ability to draw free-hand it is still possible to make an original design. An easy way to achieve this is to use cut paper shapes by folding a piece of paper in four, hold the centre folds and cut round the edges with paper-cutting scissors to form an interesting shape, avoiding too many angular corners. Place the template on to graph paper and draw round the outline lightly, square-off the rounded outlines suitable for the geometric style of canvas design. Using coloured pencils shade in the colour scheme and choose stitches appropriate to the design and scale. Alternatively, a free-hand drawing or painting can be reproduced directly on to canvas by inking the outline of the design, then lay the canvas on top of the drawing and trace the design directly on to the canvas from the black outline showing through using a fine brush and black WATERPROOF ink (or lighter colour if pale threads are to be used).

## Adapting Designs

If a chosen design requires to be adapted to fit a certain size of canvas this can be done easily if one remembers that when enlarging or reducing the scale of a design, that the increase or decrease must be done lengthwise and widthwise in proportion. The easiest method of working the scale out, is to draw the area of the original design on to a piece of tracing paper, including the outline shape of the motif or design. The diagram shows the method of enlarging or reducing the original area **a b c d**. Draw in the diagonal **a c**.

*To enlarge the area*, extend the diagonal **a c**. Extend side **a d** to the new length required at **g**. Draw in the new perpendicular from **g** to meet the diagonal at **f**. Extend side **a b** to **e** the same length as **g f**. Join **e** to **f**.

*To reduce the area*, decide on the new length of one side **a j**. Draw in the new perpendicular from **j** to meet the diagonal at **i**. Mark off the same length on **a b** at **h**. Join **h** to **i**.

Divide the original area **a b c d** into equal squares, to form a grid. If a simple or large design is used the squares can be 5 to 7.5 cm (2 to 3 in) square, if a more complex or small design is used it is advisable to use smaller squares. Whether enlarging or reducing, the new area must be subdivided exactly into the same number of squares as on the original. For easy reference the squares on each grid are identically numbered and lettered.

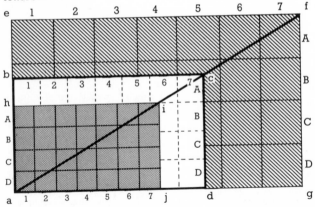

The motif or design (not shown in the plan) is now scaled up from the original drawing, each line is reproduced in the corresponding square on the new grid.

## Practical Use of Stitches

The function of the article influences the choice of stitches, threads and colours. If the article should be in practical everyday use, it is advisable to limit the range of stitchery, therefore stitches such as those with 'long arms' should be eliminated in favour of stitches which give a hard-wearing texture. A great variety of stitches is not necessary to produce an interesting piece of embroidery, two or three stitches only, used skilfully in attractive colours and threads is all that is required to create an original design. More intricate designs, such as pictures or wall hangings which are purely decorative, lend themselves to experiment with a wider range of stitchery and frequently the design may be highlighted with beads, sequins or metallic threads.

## Stretching Canvas

Before a completed tapestry can be made up, it may require to be stretched first if it has pulled slightly out of shape. DO NOT TRIM CANVAS UNTIL STRETCHING HAS BEEN COMPLETED. Stretching the canvas can be done professionally. Below we have outlined a method which could be done at home by the embroiderer.

1 Cover a firm board or wooden surface, slightly larger than the completed piece of tapestry with graph paper and draw the outline shape on the graph paper 5 cm (2 in) larger than the embroidered tapestry.

2 Cut blotting paper to size of embroidered section and place on top of graph paper to absorb moisture when dampening the tapestry.

3 It is possible to stretch the threads back to the original form by dampening the back of the tapestry and the surrounding canvas, thus softening the gum or stiffening agent. The gum or stiffening agent then dries and resets the canvas threads. The canvas must be left for two to three weeks so that the shape becomes permanent.

4 Using rustless drawing pins, pin out the canvas to size face downwards making sure that the warp and weft threads run at right angles to each other. Only if necessary, slightly dampen the worked canvas. Using the outline on the graph paper as a guide secure round all edges of the unworked canvas with drawing pins placed 6 mm (¼ in) apart parallel to the outline. The canvas may require careful pulling in order to make it square.

5 Carefully remove pins.

6 If the canvas has been very badly pulled out of shape, it may

be necessary to repeat the above process.

## Mounting of Tapestry
We suggest all needlework tapestry be professionally mounted as this gives the work a quality finish.

## Dry Cleaning
A piece of embroidery worked on canvas must always be dry cleaned or cleaned with an upholstery foam cleaner (not a carpet cleaner) and never washed as the use of water would soften the canvas.

Canvas embroidery of today can be cleaned at home, provided the embroidery threads are fast dyed. Do not remove the canvas from its mounting but clean *in situ,* this method keeps the canvas stretched while the embroidery is damp and prevents shrinkage. If the canvas is mounted as, for example, a chairseat or stool top, use a beater, brush and suction cleaner alternatively until all the dust and grit is gone. Then shampoo following the manufacturers' instructions. Place to dry in a current of air away from the sunlight.

# 50
## Needlepoint
## Stitches

# Trammed Gros Point Stitch (on Double Thread Canvas)

Fig. 1 work a Trammed Stitch (see pages 9 and 10 for working method) from left to right, then pull the needle through on the lower line; insert the needle diagonally into the upper line crossing the laid thread and 1 intersection of canvas threads (the point where a pair of narrow vertical threads cross a pair of narrow horizontal threads); bring the needle through on the lower line 2 canvas thread intersections to the left. Continue in this way to the end of the row. Fig. 2 shows the reverse side of correctly worked Gros Point Stitch where the length of the stitches is greater than those on the correct side.

Fig 1

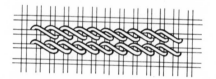

Fig 2

# Petit Point Stitch

This canvas stitch is used for fine work. There are two methods of working, either diagonal or horizontal rows of stitches, both are correct, although the former method is recommended whenever possible as it prevents the finished canvas from pulling out of shape. The diagonal method is shown at A. The rows are worked from upper left-hand corner to lower right-hand corner and vice versa. Fig. 1 shows the downward row where the stitch is worked diagonally upwards over 1 canvas thread intersection and the needle is passed vertically downwards behind 2 horizontal canvas threads and brought through in readiness for the next stitch. Fig. 2 shows the upward row, the direction of the stitches is the same as the previous row but the needle is passed horizontally behind 2 vertical canvas

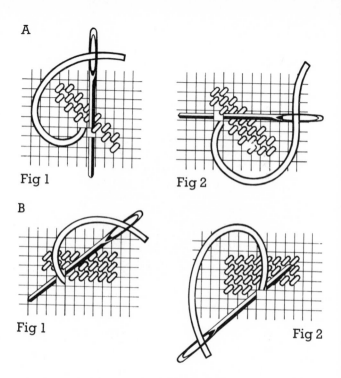

A

Fig 1

Fig 2

B

Fig 1

Fig 2

threads coming out in position for the next stitch. All stitches should slope in the same direction. The horizontal method is shown at B. The rows are worked from right to left and vice versa. Fig. 1 bring the thread out at the righthand side, work a stitch diagonally upwards over 1 canvas thread intersection, pass the needle diagonally downwards behind 1 horizontal and 2 vertical canvas threads and bring through in readiness for next stitch. Fig. 2 the second row is worked from left to right, the direction of the stitches is the same as the previous row but the needle is passed diagonally upwards. All stitches should slope in the same direction. The stitches on the reverse side are longer and slope more than on the correct side.

# Cross Stitch, Half

This is a useful stitch to use when working with a thick thread, it resembles Petit Point Stitch in appearance but the working methods are different. Half Cross Stitch consists of small diagonal stitches each worked over 1 canvas thread intersection as shown in the diagram, with the stitches on the reverse side vertical.

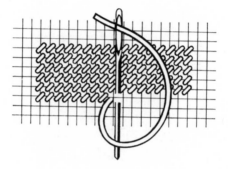

# Cross Stitch

When working Cross Stitch on canvas the correct method of working is to complete each stitch before commencing the next as shown in the diagrams. Fig. 1 bring the needle through at arrow, insert the needle at A (2 threads up and 2 threads to the left) and bring out at B (2 threads down), thus forming a half cross. Fig 2 insert the needle at C (2 threads up and 2 threads to the right) and bring out again at B, thus completing the Cross Stitch. Fig. 3 shows the completed Cross Stitch with the needle shown in position for the next stitch when working the crosses horizontally. To avoid the possibility of the canvas "pulling" the stitches may also be worked in diagonal rows. It is important when working Cross Stitch that the upper half of all crosses should lie in the same direction as shown in Fig. 4.

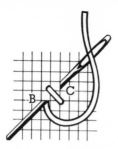

Fig 2

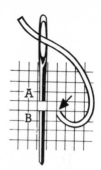

Fig 1

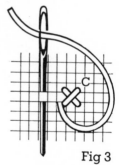

Fig 3

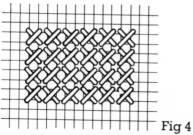

Fig 4

# Cross Stitch, Oblong

Bring the needle through at the lower right-hand side, insert the needle 4 threads up and 2 threads to the left and bring out 4 threads down, thus forming a half oblong cross, continue in this way to the end of the row. Work the other half of the cross as shown. Oblong Cross Stitch may be worked either from left to right as shown, or from right to left, but it is important that the upper half of all crosses should lie in the same direction.

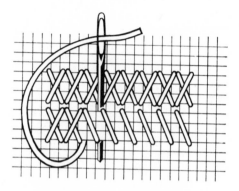

# Cross Stitch, Alternating

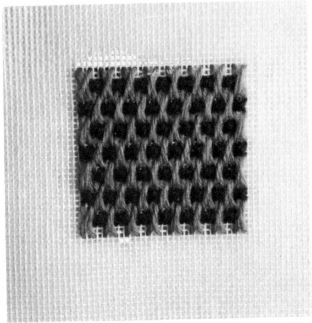

This stitch consists of Oblong Cross Stitch (see page 24 for working method) worked over 2 vertical and 6 horizontal canvas threads and Cross Stitch (see page 22 for working method) worked over 2 threads each way of the canvas. The crosses may be worked alternately from right to left as shown in Fig. 1. Alternatively the Oblong Cross Stitches may be worked first, each row overlapping the preceding row by 2 horizontal canvas threads, Cross Stitches are then worked between the previous crosses to cover the surface of the canvas either in the same colour or a contrasting colour as shown in Fig. 2.

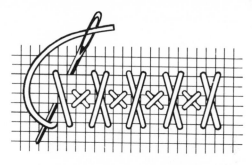

Fig 1

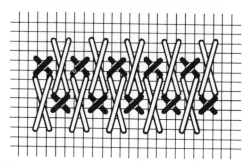

Fig 2

# Cross Stitch, Two-sided Italian

This stitch is similar in appearance on both sides of the canvas. It is worked from the bottom upwards, each row completed in two journeys working from left to right and vice versa. Fig. 1 bring the thread through at arrow; insert the needle at A (3 threads to the right) and bring out again at arrow. Fig. 2 insert the needle at B (3 threads up and 3 threads to the right) and bring out again at arrow. Fig. 3 insert the needle at C (3 threads up) and bring out again at A. Continue in this way to the end of the row. Fig. 4 passing the needle downwards behind the vertical stitches, complete the second half of each Cross Stitch as shown.

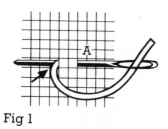

Fig 1

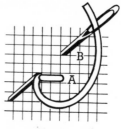

Fig 2

Fig 3

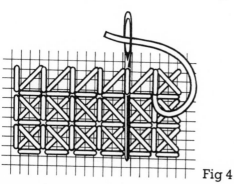

Fig 4

# Cross Stitch, Long-Armed

This stitch is worked from left to right in horizontal rows. Fig. 1 bring the thread through at arrow, insert the needle at A (3 threads up and 6 threads to the right) and bring out at B (3 threads down). Fig. 2 insert the needle at C (3 threads up and 3 threads to the left) and bring out at D (3 threads down) in readiness for the next stitch. Fig 3 shows the finished overall effect.

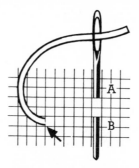

Fig 1

Fig 2
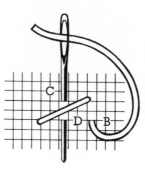

Fig 3

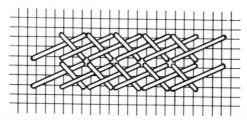

# Cross Stitch, Montenegrin

This stitch is similar in appearance to Long-Armed Cross Stitch the principal difference being the additional vertical stitches. Fig. 1 bring the thread through at arrow, insert the needle at A (4 threads up and 8 threads to the right), bring the needle through at B (4 threads down and 4 threads to the left). Fig. 2 insert the needle at C (4 threads up and 4 threads to the left), bring the needle through again at B (4 threads down and 4 threads to the right). Fig. 3 insert the needle at D (4 threads up), bring the needle through again at B (4 threads down) in readiness for the next stitch. Fig. 4 shows the finished effect.

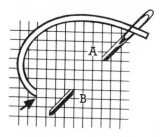

Fig 1

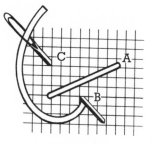

Fig 2

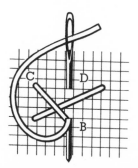

Fig 3

Continued overleaf

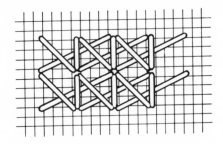

Fig 4

# Cross Stitch, Reversed

The instructions and diagrams for working the stitch illustrated above are given on the following pages.

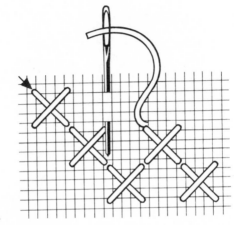

Fig 1

This stitch consists of alternating Cross Stitch and Upright Cross Stitch (see pages 22 and 38 for working methods) worked over 4 canvas threads superimposed by Cross Stitches in a contrasting colour or finer thread. Work the basic rows diagonally as shown in Fig. 1 commencing at black arrow and leaving 4 canvas threads between each row. Fig. 2 commencing at blank arrow work the Upright Cross Stitches between the rows already worked. Fig. 3 shows the finished effect with the contrasting crosses worked on top of the basic stitches.

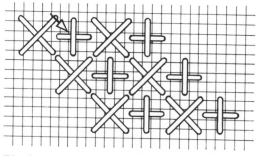

Fig 2

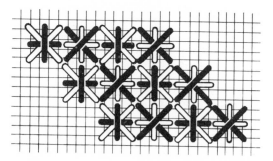

Fig 3

# Cross Stitch, Upright

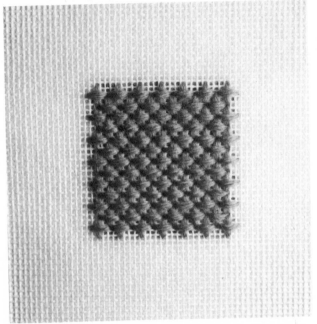

This stitch is worked diagonally from lower right to upper left corner. Fig. 1 bring the thread out at arrow; insert the needle at A (4 threads up) and bring out at B (2 threads down and 2 threads to the left). Continue in this way to the end of the row. Fig. 2 after completing the last stitch, bring the needle through as if to commence a further stitch. Insert the needle at C (4 threads to the right) and bring it through at D (2 threads down and 2 threads to the left). Continue in this way to the end of the row.

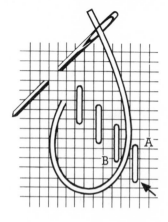

Fig 1

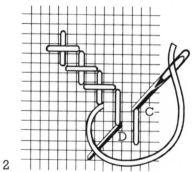

Fig 2

39

# Cross Stitch, Double

This stitch forms a square over 4 horizontal and 4 vertical threads of canvas. Fig. 1 work a Cross Stitch as shown; then bring the needle through 4 threads down and 2 threads to the left. Fig. 2 insert the needle 4 threads up and bring through 2 threads to the left and 2 threads down. Fig. 3 insert the needle 4 threads to the right and bring through 2 threads down and 4 threads to the left in readiness to commence the next stitch. For the overall effect it is important when working an area of Double Cross Stitch that the last upper stitch of each should lie in the same direction.

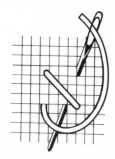

Fig 1

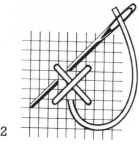

Fig 2

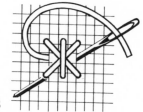

Fig 3

# Cross Stitch, Diagonal

This stitch is worked diagonally from lower right to upper left corner. Fig. 1 bring the thread through at arrow, insert the needle at A (4 threads up) and bring out again at arrow. Fig. 2 insert the needle at B (2 threads up and 2 threads to the right) and bring through again at C (4 threads to the left). Fig. 3 insert the needle again at B (4 threads to the right) and bring through again at C (4 threads to the left) in readiness for the next stitch. Continue in this way to the end of the row.

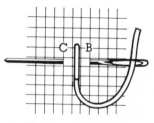

Fig 2

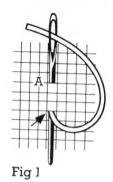

Fig 1

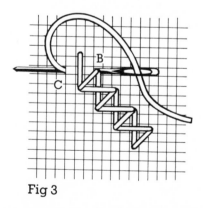

Fig 3

# Rice Stitch

This stitch is usually worked in a thick embroidery thread for the large Cross Stitch (see page 22 for working method) and a finer thread for the small Back Stitch. Fig. 1 first, cover the required area with Cross Stitch worked over 4 threads each way of the canvas. Fig. 2 over the corners of each Cross Stitch work small diagonal Back Stitches at right angles over 2 threads each way of the canvas, so that these small stitches also form a cross. The small stitches have been shown in black in order to show the construction. Fig. 3 shows the finished overall effect.

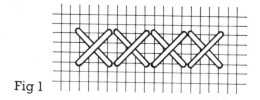

Fig 1

Fig 2

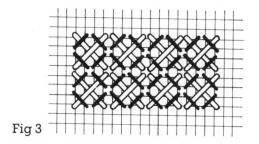

Fig 3

# Gobelin Stitch, Straight

There are two methods of working this stitch. Fig. 1 shows the method where a very close effect is desired. Work a Trammed Stitch first from left to right (see pages 9 and 10 Split Trammed Stitch), then pull the needle through 1 thread down and 1 thread to the left and insert again 2 threads above. Pull the needle through 2 threads down and 1 to the left in readiness for the next stitch. Fig. 2 shows the method of working minus the laid thread. This method although similar in effect to the first method is thinner and therefore less hard-wearing.

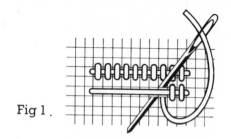

Fig 1.

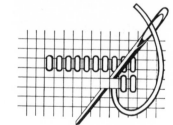

Fig 2

# Gobelin Stitch, Encroaching

This stitch gives a very close fabric effect, ideal for shading. The stitches are worked in rows from right to left and vice versa. Each stitch is worked over 5 horizontal canvas threads and diagonally over 1 vertical canvas thread. On completion of the first row, work the following rows in the same way, each row overlapping the previous row by 1 horizontal canvas thread.

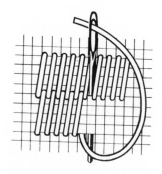

# Gobelin Stitch, Filling

This stitch consists of Straight Stitches worked in rows alternately from left to right and right to left. Commence the first row by bringing the thread through at arrow and make a row of stitches over 6 canvas threads leaving 2 threads between each. The second row is worked from right to left and the stitches fit evenly into the previous row as shown in diagram. Continue working each successive row in this way. The spaces left on first and last rows may be filled with Straight Stitches worked over 3 canvas threads.

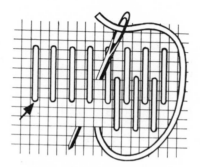

# Gobelin Stitch, Plaited

This stitch is worked in horizontal rows of diagonal straight stitches the direction of each row alternating and arranged to overlap the preceding row to give a plaited or woven effect. Fig. 1 bring the thread through at arrow, insert the needle at A (4 threads up and 2 threads to the left), bring the needle through at B (4 threads down); continue in this way to the end of the row. Fig. 2 on completion of the last stitch of the first row, bring the needle through at C (6 threads down), insert the needle at D as shown (4 threads up and 2 threads to the right), bring the needle through at E (4 threads down); continue in this way to the end of the row overlapping the stitches in the previous row. Fig. 3 shows the finished plaited effect.

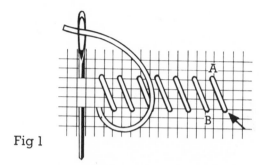

Fig 1

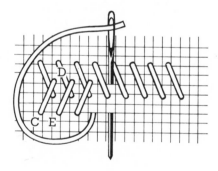

Fig 2

Continued overleaf

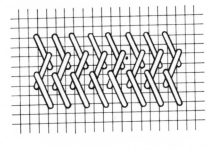

 Fig 3

# Knotted Stitch

The instructions and diagrams for working the stitch illustrated above are given on the following pages.

**Knotted Stitch (continued)**

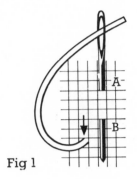

**Fig 1**

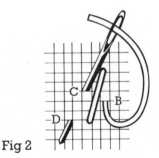

**Fig 2**

This stitch is worked in horizontal rows from right to left. Fig. 1 bring the thread through at arrow and insert the needle at A (6 threads up and 2 threads to the right), bring the needle out at B (4 threads down). Fig. 2 insert the needle at C (2 threads up and 2 threads to the left), bring the needle through at D

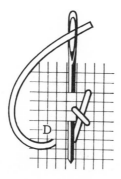

**Fig 3**

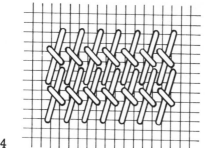

**Fig 4**

(4 threads down and 2 threads to the left). Fig. 3 shows the completed stitch and the needle in position for the next stitch. Fig. 4 shows two rows of stitches, the second row fitting evenly into the preceding row.

# Fishbone Stitch

This stitch is worked diagonally in vertical rows, the direction of each row alternating to give a zig-zag effect. Fig. 1 bring the thread through at arrow, insert the needle at A (6 threads up and 6 threads to the right), bring the needle through at B (2 threads to the left). Fig. 2 insert the needle at C (2 threads down and 2 threads to the right) overlapping the previous stitch just made, bring the needle through at D (6 threads down and 6 threads to the left) in readiness for the next stitch. Continue in this way to the end of the row. Work the next and every alternate row at right angles to the preceding row to form the zig-zag pattern as shown in Fig. 3.

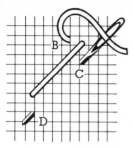

Fig 2

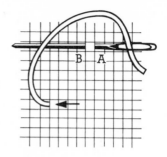

Fig 1

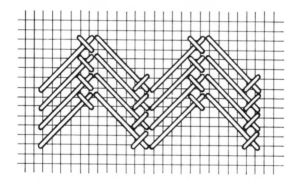

Fig 3

# Hungarian Stitch

This stitch may be worked in one or two colours. It consists of rows of vertical Straight Stitches worked in sequence over 2, 4 and 2 horizontal threads of canvas, leaving 2 vertical threads between each group of stitches. Each row is set alternately into the preceding row as shown in the diagram.

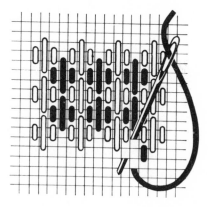

# Hungarian Stitch, Variation

This stitch consists of rows of vertical Straight Stitches worked in sequence over 2, 4, 6 and 4 horizontal threads of canvas. Each row is set alternately into the preceding row as shown in diagram.

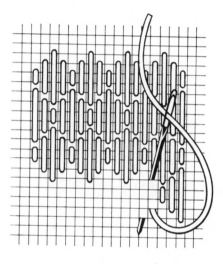

# Parisian Stitch

This stitch, which may be worked from right to left or left to right, consists of Straight Stitches alternately worked over 6 and 2 horizontal threads of canvas. Each row is worked alternating the length of the stitches to fit into the preceding row, as shown in diagram.

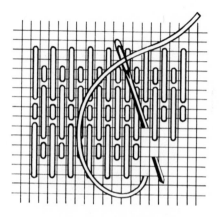

# Florentine Stitch

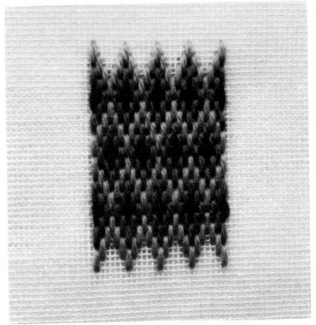

This stitch is used for working zig-zag patterns known as Florentine work. It is generally used to fill a large area and is then worked in two or more rows of different colours forming an all over wave pattern. The size of the wave may be varied, depending upon the number of stitches or the number of threads over which the stitches are worked. Fig. 1 shows the method of working a single row of stitches. Fig. 2 shows the finished effect when using three colours.

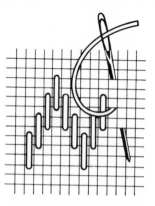

Fig 1

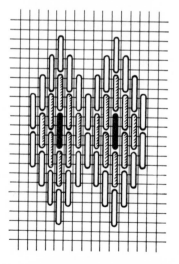

Fig 2

# Long Stitch

This stitch consists of two rows of vertical Straight Stitches worked from right to left or left to right in sequence over 4, 3, 2, 1, 2 and 3 horizontal canvas threads to form a triangular pattern. The second row of stitches, worked in reverse sequence 1, 2, 3, 4, 3 and 2 canvas threads fit evenly into the preceding row to from a parallel  band. Continue working these two rows in the same way for the finished effect, as shown.

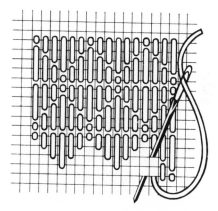

# Long Stitch, Variation

This variation consists of three rows of vertical Straight Stitches worked from right to left or left to right to form a wave pattern. The first row is worked over 4 horizontal canvas threads, the second and third rows are each worked over 2 horizontal canvas threads. Continue working these three rows in sequence following the diagram for the finished effect, as shown.

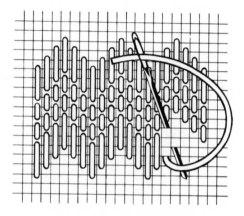

# Jacquard Stitch

This stitch is used to produce a woven fabric or brocaded effect on large areas. The rows of stitches are shown in two colours to show the construction clearly but one colour only may be used depending on the desired effect. The rows of stitches are arranged to give an even "stepped" effect. Rows of stitches are worked diagonally from upper left to lower right and vice versa each row is completed before commencing the next. The length of stitches alternate, one row the stitches are worked diagonally over 2 canvas thread intersections, the next row over 1 canvas thread intersection.

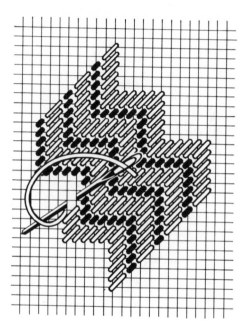

# Jacquard Stitch, Variation

This stitch is used to produce a woven fabric or brocaded effect on large areas. Similar to Jacquard Stitch the rows are arranged to give an even "stepped" effect. The rows of stitches are worked diagonally from upper right to lower left and vice versa and the length of the stitches, in the alternating rows, worked diagonally over 2 and 4 canvas thread intersections.

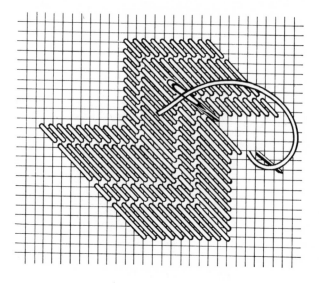

# Byzantine Stitch

This stitch is used to produce a woven fabric or brocaded effect. It consists of Satin Stitches worked diagonally over 4 vertical and 4 horizontal canvas threads to create a woven "stepped" effect as shown.

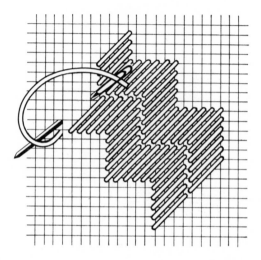

# Diagonal Stitch

This stitch gives the effect of woven fabric or brocade when worked over a large surface area. Fig. 1 shows the method of working. Bring the thread through at arrow and work Straight Stitches over 2, 3, 4 and 3 intersections of canvas threads as shown. Continue working in this way to the end of the row. Fig. 2 shows the position of the following rows in relation to the first, where the longest stitches of one row fall diagonally below the shortest stitches of the previous row.

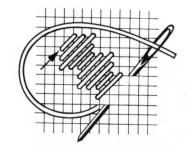

Fig 1

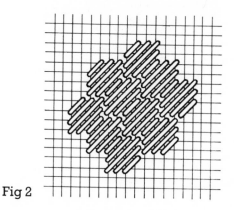

Fig 2

# Milanese Stitch

This stitch is used to produce a woven fabric or brocaded effect on large areas. The triangular pattern consists of four stitches of graded length set in diagonal rows alternately pointing upwards and downwards. The basic stitch used throughout is Back Stitch worked from right to left. Bring the thread through at arrow, insert the needle at A (1 thread up and 1 thread to the right) and bring out at B (5 threads down and 5 threads to the left), insert the needle again at arrow (4 threads up and 4 threads to the right) and bring out at C (5 threads down and 5 threads to the left), insert the needle again at B (1 thread up and 1 thread to the right) and bring out at D (5 threads down and 5 threads to the left) and insert the needle again at C (4 threads up and 4 threads to the right). Continue in this way to the end

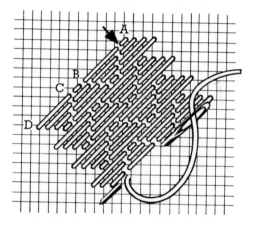

of the row. For each of the remaining three rows of the pattern work Back Stitches over 2 and 3, 3 and 2, 4 and 1 canvas thread intersections. Continue working in this sequence to achieve the desired effect.

# Cashmere Stitch

This stitch is used to produce a woven fabric or brocaded effect on large areas. The pattern consists of diagonal stitches worked in sequence over 1, 2 and 2 canvas intersections with the lower end of each stitch falling exactly beneath the other and the unit of three stitches moving 1 thread to the right each time when working diagonally downwards from left to right. Similarly, the unit moves 1 thread to the left when working upwards from right to left as shown in the diagram.

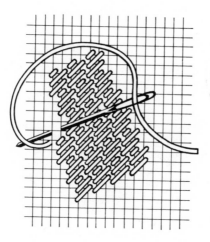

# Moorish Stitch

This stitch is used to produce a woven fabric or brocaded effect. It consists of rows of diagonal stitches worked from top left to lower righthand corner. The stitches are worked in sequence over 2, 4, 6 and 4 canvas thread intersections with alternate rows of small stitches worked to give a "stepped" effect, each stitch is worked over 2 canvas thread intersections.

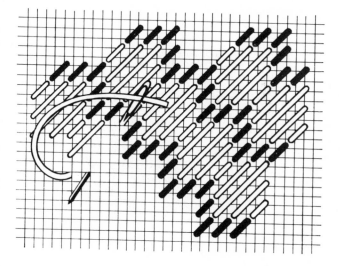

# Star Stitch

This stitch forms a square over 6 horizontal and 6 vertical threads of canvas. It consists of eight Straight Stitches worked over 3 canvas threads, each worked from the outer edge into the same central hole as shown in the diagram and worked in horizontal or vertical rows.

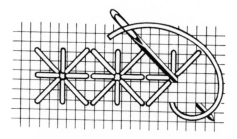

# Star Stitch on Squared Background

This stitch is used for filling large areas and consists of individual Star Stitches worked over 6 horizontal and 6 vertical threads of canvas (see page 86 for working method) and outlined with Petit Point Stitch worked over 1 intersection of canvas threads (see page 18 for working method). The stitches are shown in two colours to show the construction clearly, but one colour only may be used depending on the desired effect.

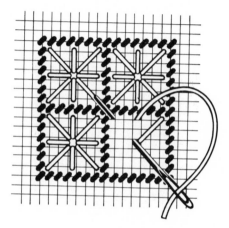

# Scottish Stitch

This stitch is used for filling large areas to give a woven fabric effect. The stitches are shown in two colours to show the construction clearly, but one colour only may be used depending on the desired effect. The Satin Stitch Squares are worked first, comprising of stitches worked diagonally across 1, 2, 3, 4, 3, 2 and 1 intersections of canvas threads as shown. The squares are outlined with Petit Point Stitch worked over 1 intersection of canvas threads.

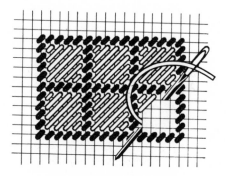

# Chequer Stitch

This stitch is used to produce a woven fabric effect. The pattern consists of alternating squares of Satin Stitch and Petit Point Stitch (see page 18 for working method), each square worked over 4 horizontal and 4 vertical threads of canvas. The easiest method of working this stitch is to work the squares in diagonal rows commencing at the upper left-hand corner, this is especially useful when working in two shades of thread as shown in the diagram.

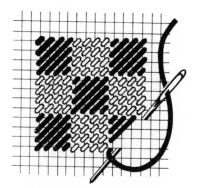

# Plait Stitch

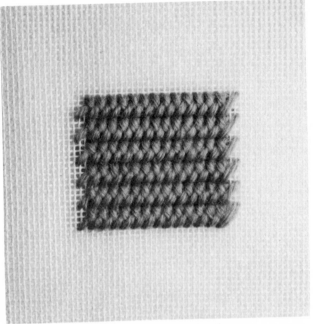

This stitch is worked in horizontal rows from left to right. It resembles Plaited Algerian Stitch (see page 97) in appearance although the working method differs. Fig. 1 bring the thread through at arrow and insert the needle at A (4 threads up and 4 threads to the right) and bring the needle out at B (4 threads down). Fig. 2 insert the needle at C (4 threads up and 2 threads to the left) and bring the needle out at D (4 threads down). Fig. 3 shows the completed stitch and the needle in position for the next stitch. Fig. 4 shows two rows of completed stitches.

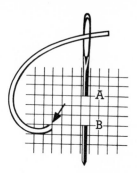

Fig 1

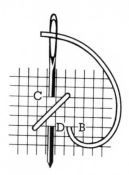

Fig 2

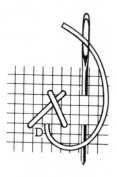

Fig 3

Continued overleaf

Plait Stitch (continued)

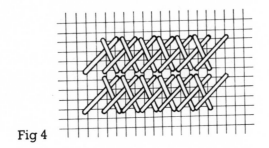

Fig 4

# Algerian Stitch, Plaited

The instructions and diagrams for working the stitch illustrated
above are given on the following pages.

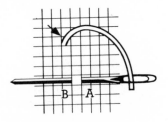

Fig 1

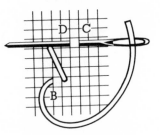

Fig 2

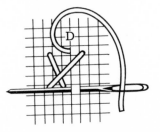

Fig 3

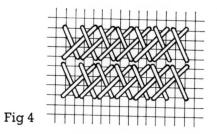

Fig 4

This stitch is worked in horizontal rows from left to right. It resembles Plait Stitch (see page 94) in appearance although the working method differs. Fig. 1 bring the thread through at arrow and insert the needle at A (4 threads down and 2 threads to the right) and bring the needle out at B (2 threads to the left). Fig. 2 insert the needle at C (4 threads up and 4 threads to the right) and bring the needle out at D (2 threads to the left). Fig. 3 shows the completed stitch and the needle in position for the next stitch. Fig. 4 shows two rows of completed stitches.

# Chain Stitch

This stitch is worked in vertical rows commencing at the top. Bring the thread out between 2 canvas threads and hold it down with the left thumb. Insert the needle into the same hole where thread emerged and bring needle out two canvas threads down and draw through the loop just made. Continue in this way to the bottom of the row finishing off the last stitch with a small straight stitch into the same hole. When used as a filling leave 2 canvas threads between each row of stitches.

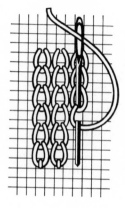

# Renaissance Stitch

This stitch consists of a group of 3 stitches worked in vertical rows although the finished appearance gives a horizontal ribbed effect. Fig. 1 bring the thread through at arrow, insert the needle at A (2 threads to the left) and bring through at B (1 thread down). Fig. 2 insert the needle at C (2 threads up) and bring through at D (2 threads down and 1 thread to the right). Fig. 3 insert the needle at E (2 threads up) and bring through at F (3 threads down and 1 thread to the right) in readiness for the next stitch (see Fig. 4). Fig. 4 shows the beginning of a stitch and the finished effect of a few completed rows.

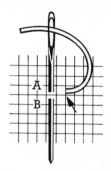

**Fig 1**

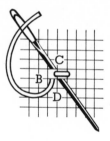

**Fig 2**

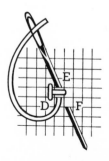

**Fig 3**

Continued overleaf

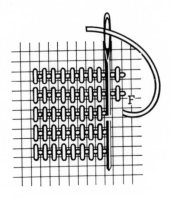

Fig 4

# Knitting Stitch

The instructions and diagrams for working the stitch illustrated above are given on the following pages.

## Knitting Stitch (continued)

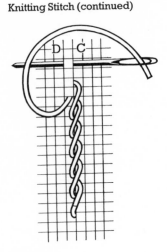

**Fig 2**

**Fig 1**

This stitch closely resembles the right side of stocking stitch knitting and is also similar in appearance to Chain Stitch (see page 100). Fig. 1 commencing at the bottom of the row bring the thread through at arrow, insert needle at A (4 threads up and 1 thread to the right), bring the needle through at B (2 threads down and 1 thread to the left); continue in this way to end of the row. Fig. 2 finish off the last stitch of the first row by inserting the needle at C, bring through at D (2 threads to the left) in readiness for the next row. Fig. 3 shows the working of the downward row. Fig. 4 shows the finished knitting effect.

Fig 3

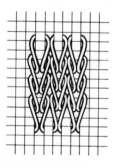

Fig 4

# Stem Stitch

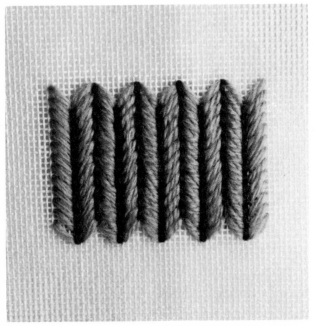

This stitch consists of oblique Straight Stitches worked in vertical rows. The direction of the stitches in alternate rows are worked at right angles to each other over 4 canvas thread intersections, to form a zig-zag pattern as shown in Fig. 1. To complete the effect small Back Stitches, over 2 canvas threads, are worked vertically between each vertical row of slanting Straight Stitches as shown in Fig. 2.

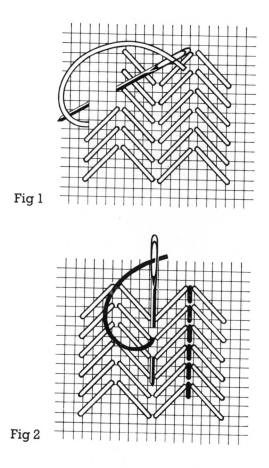

Fig 1

Fig 2

# Eastern Stitch

This stitch is worked in rows from left to right. Fig. 1 bring the thread through at arrow, insert the needle at A (4 threads to the right), bring the needle through at B (4 threads down and 4 to the left). Fig. 2 insert the needle again at arrow (4 threads up), bring the thread through at C (4 threads down and 4 to the right).

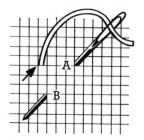

Fig 1

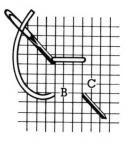

Fig 2

Continued overleaf

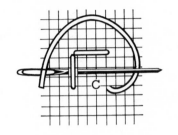

**Fig 3**

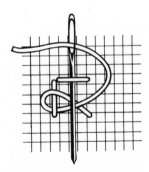

**Fig 4**

Fig. 3 pass the needle from left to right under the vertical stitch without piercing the canvas, keep the working thread under the needle and pull the thread through to form a twisted loop. Fig. 4 pass the needle downwards under the horizontal stitch

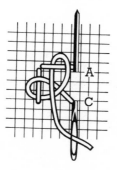

**Fig 5**

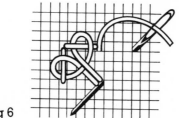

**Fig 6**

without piercing the canvas again keeping the working thread under the needle and pull to form another twisted loop. Fig. 5 insert the needle again at C, bring the thread out again at A. Fig. 6 shows one completed Eastern Stitch.

# Rhodes Stitch

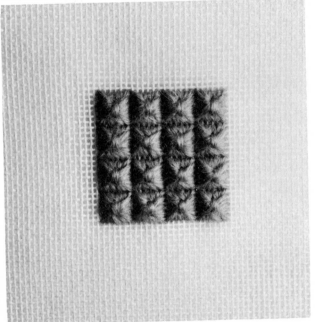

This is an attractive raised filling stitch which covers a square of canvas with an even number of threads. The working method is the same whatever the number of canvas threads making up the square. Fig. 1 shows the construction of a Rhodes Stitch over a square of 6 horizontal and 6 vertical threads. Bring the thread through at A, insert the needle at B, bring through at C, insert at D, bring through at E, insert at F. Continue in this way following the direction of the arrows, each stitch overlapping the previous stitch until square is filled. Finish off with a small vertical Straight Stitch at centre taken through the layers of thread and canvas as shown in Fig. 2.

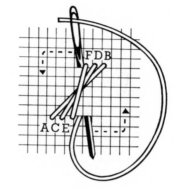

Fig 1

Fig 2

# Fern Stitch

This stitch is worked from the top downwards. Bring the thread through at arrow, insert the needle 4 threads down and 4 threads to the right and bring out 2 threads to the left, insert the needle 4 threads up and 4 threads to the right, bring out 1 thread down and 6 threads to the left in readiness for the next stitch.

# Fan Stitch

This stitch consists of five or nine Straight Stitches, depending on the thickness of thread used, which cover 4 horizontal and 4 vertical threads of canvas all radiating outwards from the same hole to form a square as shown in Fig. 1. Fan Stitch may be worked in horizontal or vertical rows, with the "fan" shapes all lying in the same direction or alternating as shown in Fig. 2.

Fig 1

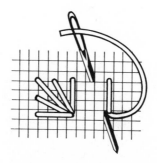

Fig 2

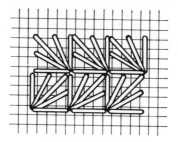

# Shell Stitch

This stitch consists of a cluster of Straight Stitches caught at the middle with a Back Stitch to form a "sheaf", the sheaves are then linked together with a coiled thread in a contrasting colour to form a border or series of borders. Fig. 1 bring the thread through at arrow, insert the needle at A (6 threads up) and bring through at B (1 thread to the left). Fig. 2 insert the needle at C (6 threads down) and bring through at D (1 thread to the left).

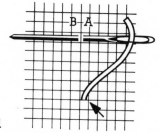

Fig 1

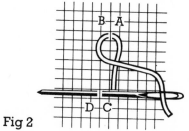

Fig 2

Continued overleaf

## Shell Stitch (continued)

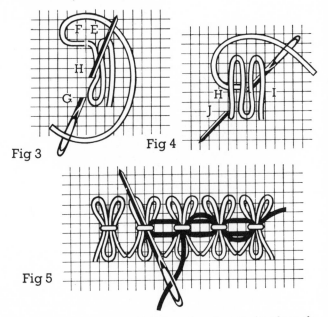

Fig 3

Fig 4

Fig 5

Fig. 3 insert the needle at E (6 threads up) and bring through at F (1 thread to the left) insert the needle at G (6 threads down) and bring through at H (3 threads up and 1 thread to the right). Fig. 4 insert the needle at I (1 thread to the right) and bring through at J (3 threads down and 3 threads to the left) in readiness for the next stitch. Fig. 5 on completion of the "sheaves", link them together by coiling the contrasting thread through the surface Back Stitches as shown. Commence at the right-hand side, pass the needle downwards through the first Back Stitch, upwards through the second Back Stitch, downwards through the first stitch again, upwards through the second, then downwards through the third, upwards through the second. Continue in this way to the end of the row. If desired, Back Stitches over 3 vertical threads of canvas may be worked in the contrasting colour between each border row.

# Velvet Stitch

This stitch resembles the pile of an Oriental carpet. It is worked from left to right in rows working from the bottom upwards. Fig. 1 bring the thread through at arrow and insert the needle at A (2 threads up and 2 threads to the right), bring out again at the arrow; re-insert the needle at A leaving a loop of thread at the bottom (the loops may be worked over a thick knitting needle to regulate the length) bring the needle out at B (2 threads down), insert at C (2 threads up and 2 threads to the left), bring out again at B in readiness for the next stitch. After all the rows have been worked (the effect is shown in Fig. 2), the loops are cut and trimmed evenly to the desired length, care must be taken not to trim the tufts too short.

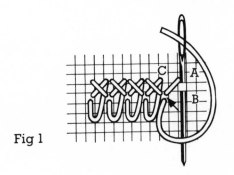

Fig 1

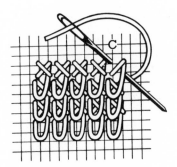

Fig 2

# Knotted Stitch, Single

This stitch closely resembles carpet knotting and gives a rich pile or fringe effect which adds a luxurious texture to canvas embroidery. The stitches may be worked singly or in rows working from left to right and from the bottom row upwards, leaving 1 or 2 horizontal canvas threads between each row. Fig. 1 insert the needle at arrow on the right side of canvas, leaving a short length of thread held down by the left thumb, bring the needle through at A (1 thread up and 2 threads to the left), insert the needle at B (3 threads to the right) and bring through C (1 thread down and 2 threads to the left). Fig. 2 continue pulling the lefthand thread firmly downwards until a tight knot is made.

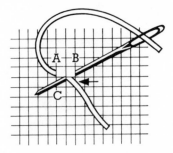

Fig 1

Fig 2

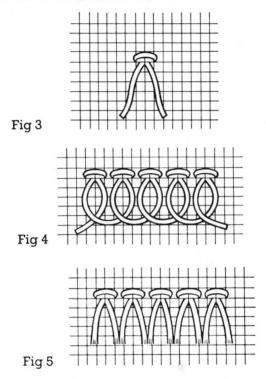

Fig 3

Fig 4

Fig 5

Fig. 3 if one stitch only is required, trim the loose threads to a suitable length at this stage. If a row of stitches is worked, omit stage 3 and continue working as shown in fig. 4 forming loops between each stitch (the loops may be worked over a thick knitting needle or ruler to regulate the length). Fig. 4 cut the loops and trim evenly to form a fringe as shown in Fig. 5 or to the desired length. If several rows are to be worked it is advisable to trim the loops last, to achieve an even pile. Care must be taken not to trim the tufts too short.

## Alphabetical Index

"Thank you good folks for allowing us to serve you, and for your loyal support in using our Readco Republic Rubber Printing Plates, and most of all for your friendship and the pleasant business relations which we enjoy with you."

From the point of view of necessary business operation, the writing of the above letter was a pure waste of time; from the point of view of giving a good customer a pleasant little surprise, it may have been the most productive letter mailed that day by the Republic Engraving and Designing Co.

No matter the cause given by your letter, your true purpose is added goodwill and regard both for and from your customers. Every bridge between you will eventually reap a reward as both your image and your income soar.

**Here's something "interesting," friend!** Speaking of the good that can be accomplished by letters with no business purpose other than to carry a little goodwill, R.W. Baxandall once said: "For building goodwill and overcoming sales resistance, one of the best ideas we ever have used is to send the customer or prospect some idea or information he can use in his own business, saying that we are sending it with our compliments, and hope that he will find it useful. Such thoughtfulness, *with no strings attached*, is appreciated by the recipient. It shows that the writer knows his problems, and is interested in helping him."

After the above introduction, Mr. Baxandall illustrated his thought with a number of pertinent examples.

- A bank sends business firms a reprint of a timely speech on current financial problems.

- A college sends to high school principals a "school calendar" with spaces for filling in the social and athletic activities for each day of the school year.

- A printer sends a football schedule for colleges in the state.

- A jeweler sends an inexpensive "Memory Book" to high school graduates.

- A department store sends a "Baby Book" to parents of newborn babies.

- A manufacturer sends his customers a mimeographed list of government publications which may be helpful to them.

- A popcorn company in Iowa sends its customers ideas on how others are getting business—the best locations, etc.